MW01122173

BIRTHSIGNS
from the Celtic Animal Year

BIRTHSIGNS
the celtic animal year

Molly Gowen and Lavinia Hamer

TOWN HOUSE

Published in 1993 by
Town House and Country House
42 Morehampton Road
Donnybrook
Dublin 4
Ireland

A CIP catalogue record for this book is available from
the British Library.

ISBN: 0-948524-62-6

Managing editor: Treasa Coady
Text editor: Elaine Campion
Book design: Bill Murphy
Printed in Hong Kong

Contents

Preface

This work is an introduction to the wealth of beauty, magic and spirituality contained in the folklore and mythology of the Celtic tradition, a tradition that is as rich and diverse as that of Greece, Rome and Egypt.

Long before the development of the Roman calendar that we use today, the Celts used animals and trees to describe their year. Each month of the year was associated with particular animals, trees, deities, colours and so forth, and this was all part of the Celts' religious system that has been passed down in an oral tradition spanning three thousand years.

This book brings together many of the myths and legends that surround the sacred animals of the Celtic year, which I have arranged within an astrological framework. Readers will find here a novel approach to studying their birth sign, which will be revealed through illustrations, Celtic deities, animals, and personal attributes. I have included a Glossary to assist the reader with unfamiliar terms.

It is important to remember that mythology by its nature is imprecise, and that traditions and beliefs tend to overlap or differ slightly from one country to the next. There are often equivalent gods in the different traditions, known by different names and with different stories surrounding them. Or there may be several conflicting myths surrounding the same deity, which is not surprising given that the stories have generally been handed down by word of mouth. The stories included here are but one version. I have also included a Glossary for further information and elucidation of unfamiliar terms.

As with its companion work, *Birthsigns from the Celtic Tree Year* (Town House, 1993), this was very much a shared project, and I am indebted to my dear friend and colleague Vin, whose enchanting artwork defies description. The experience of working with Vin has been a pleasure, a privilege and an inspiration. I hope readers will get as much pleasure from reading this book and enjoying the artwork as we got from creating it.

I dedicate this book to my dear friend Donald Tripp, RIP, and to my astrological consultant, the wonderful Sandra Cooper-Sutton. Love and thanks to Sr Bernard Sheehan, my godmother, and to my parents John and Margaret Gowen for their continued love and support. Thanks also to Seán Wyse Jackson and to my children Rory and Dawn Fiona.

Molly Gowen
May 1993

Personal attributes:

Achieving, responsible, earthy.
Sometimes arrogant, rigid, insensitive.

The **Deer** is ruled by the planet Saturn.
Its element is Earth. (See p 32.)

Cailte* speaks:

Cold it is, winter and the wind
  rising:
The great red stag is raging.
No shelter here on this barren
  crag:
This feeds his temper.

The stag of Sliabh Carn, our
  council place,
Can not lie down for the cold.
The stamping stag of Echtga
  Head
Is listening to the wolves'
  music.

I, Cailte, with fair Diarmaid
And Oscar, valiant and slight,
Have felt the east winds
  keening
Through many a long night.

* Cailte was a cousin of Fionn
mac Cumhaill, leader of the
Fianna.

(Adapted from 12th C. Fenian
poems by M Gowen)

This is the month of the
deer, symbol of nobility and
kingship.

Deer in many guises appear
in several mythologies. The
hind was sacred to the moon
goddess Diana in Greece,
while Artemis, the huntress,
had a white roebuck in her
grove in Arcadia. (The
roebuck in the thicket was
also a symbol of the ancient
druidic mysteries.) The
Phoenicians worshipped a
white antelope, whose ribs
they used to make the
curved sides of their lyres. In
the Celtic tradition, fawns
are connected with the
Otherworld, known as Tír
na nÓg (Land of Youth) in
Ireland and the Land of
Annwm in Wales.

Worship of the stag was a
very ancient and widespread
practice. He appears as the
Celtic Cernunnos (the
horned one) or Pan, the
Green Man of the Forest, a
deity of both death and
regeneration.

'Suibne is no proper name for me,
Horn Head now I favour.'
(Attributed to Suibne Geilt, 12th C. Irish)

Suibne Geilt, Lord of Transformations and a Merlin-type figure in the Irish tradition, is another version of this deity, as he is Lord of the Stags in one of his incarnations.

The god King Llew in the Welsh tales is in the form of a stag when he is killed by his dark twin, Gronw Pebyr (a figure of evil personified). Llew's medieval successor,

Red Robin Hood, was also worshipped in the form of a stag that grew a red coat in the summer.

Personal attributes:
Objective, thinking, friendly.
Sometimes loner, eccentric, rebellious.

The **Heron** is ruled by the planet Uranus.
Its element is Air. (See p 32.)

From 'The Stolen Child'

Where dips the rocky highland
Of Sleuth Wood in the lake,
There lies a leafy island
Where flapping herons wake
The drowsy water-rats;
There we've hid our faery vats,
Full of berries
And of reddest stolen cherries.
Come away, O human child!
To the waters and the wild
With a faery, hand in hand,
For the world's more full of
   weeping than you can
   understand.

Where the wave of moonlight
   glosses
The dim grey sands with light,
Far off by furthest Rosses,
We foot it all the night,
Weaving olden dances,
Mingling hands and mingling
   glances
Till the moon has taken flight;
To and fro we leap
And chase the frothy bubbles,
While the world is full of
   troubles
And is anxious in its sleep.
Come away, O human child!
To the waters and the wild
With a faery, hand in hand,
For the world's more full of
   weeping than you can
   understand.

(W B Yeats, 1865–1939)

This is the month of the heron. All seabirds were revered by the ancient Irish as messengers to the Otherworld, but the crane and heron were also associated with wisdom.

In Ireland Manannán Mac Lir, the sea-god, carried the treasures of the sea, that is, the culture and language of the Milesians, in a bag made from crane skin. These treasures are also described as the wisdom of the Beth-Luis-Nion, the ogham alphabet. This alphabet was called after the first three trees in the old Celtic tree calendar: Beth the birch, Luis the rowan, and Nion the ash. The letters BLN are the first of the thirteen consonants of the ogham alphabet.

The flight of cranes was reputed to have inspired the Roman god Mercury to invent the alphabet. The ibis, a similar bird, was revered by Etruscans and Egyptians, to whose deity, Thoth, this bird was sacred. Thoth was the inventor of

10

Three herons guarded the entrance to the dark castle of the Otherworld, crying ceaselessly 'Beware! Beware! Do not enter! Pass by!'

writing and the god who reformed the Egyptian calendar.

On Manannán's Island, the Isle of Man, three herons guard the entrance to the Otherworld ruled by Midir the Proud. This is reminiscent of the cave of Cruachan in south-western Ireland and the cave at the mouth of the Styx in Greece.

Cranes are no longer native to Ireland, but herons are to be found wherever water flows. Herons are also held to be sacred because of their habit of arranging the fish they catch to form a wheel, symbol of the charioteer Lugh Lámhfhada — like Apollo, a god of enlightenment and civilisation.

11

Personal attributes:
Artistic, spiritual, supersensitive.
Sometimes confused, undisciplined, escapist.

The **Fish** is ruled by the planet Nepturn.
Its element is Water. (See p 32.)

Amerghin the Druid came from Spain with the Milesians and this is part of the invocation he uttered on first landing on Irish soil.

Who carves the cragginess of
  mountains?
Who but myself knows where
  the sun shall set?
Who but myself knows the ages
  of the moon?
Who summons cattle from the
  house of Tethra*?
On whom do the cattle of
  Tethra* smile?
Whose forge lies under the
  sacred hill?

Fish full seas
Of Inisfáil.*
Streams of fish
Weave through the deep.
Birds in flight
Through the great ocean.

Glittering torrent,
Salmon swift,
Their music breaks
The surface silence.

* Tethra = the undersea god of
   the Fomorians
* Cattle of Tethra = fish
* Inisfáil = Ireland

This is the month of the spring equinox, associated always with fish. The whale dolphin and sturgeon were royal fish in Britain, while the salmon was king of the fish in Ireland.

The dolphin has long been considered an oracular fish in Greece (the Greek word *delphis* means 'dolphin'). The Greek sun-god Apollo often appeared in this form, and the frisking of dolphins is still generally held to portend a storm.

In the Christian tradition Jesus was symbolised as a fish, the holy Ichthus, and the Ark of the Covenant was said to have been covered with dolphin skin.

In the Welsh tradition the moon goddess Arianrhod had three sons: the divine child Dylan (the wave), Llew Llaw, and Gywn (the white one). Dylan is also called Silver Fish and is associated with the Great Flood.

(Adapted by M Gowen)

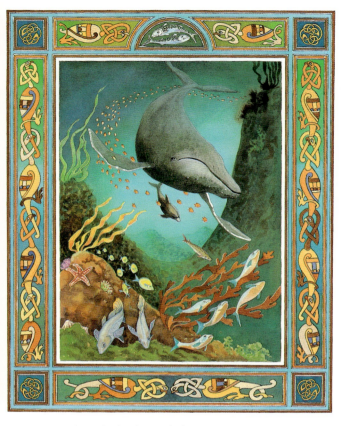

'On whom do the cattle of Tethra smile?'

In Ireland, Finntain the Bard
as the Salmon of Knowledge
roamed the wide ocean until
the subsidence of the Great
Flood, when he resumed his
role as tutelary deity to the
Ollav poets.

Personal attributes:

Innovative, individualistic, achieving.
Sometimes withdrawn, restless, intolerant.

The **Bear** is ruled by the planet Mars.
Its element is Fire. (See p 32.)

The study of astronomy was an integral part of the cultures of all ancient peoples, including the Celts. To north European people the sky was dominated by the constellations Ursa Major and Ursa Minor (the Great She Bear and the Little She Bear). These stars seem to rotate around the pivotal Pole Star, which lies directly above the North Pole. This was considered to be the celestial hinge (the 'cardo') around which the universe revolved. The Greek deity Eurynome, also known as Artemis Calliste, was believed to preside over this hinge. She was known as Cardea to the Celts and she gives her name to the cardinal winds, virtues, etc.

Another god who belongs to this region beyond the winter stars is Boreas, the North Wind, a deity honoured all over Europe. His people, the Hyperboreans, were probably worshippers of the North Wind in the Eastern tradition.

Bears were sacred to the 'Great Goddess' in many cultures. In early Europe, figurines in the shape of bears were placed in the cribs of newborn babies so that they would be under the protection of the Great Mother Bear. This is probably one of the origins of the Teddy Bear.

King Arthur is apparently a form of the bear god Artios or Artiaus, about whom little is known except that he is a figure of the greatest antiquity. Artios was consort to Cerridwen, the Welsh triple goddess who possessed a magic cauldron. In the medieval Welsh romance of Culhwch and Olwen, we hear how Arthur went to Ireland to recover this cauldron and 'laid waste to one of the five provinces'.

14

Mother and baby European brown bear under the 'Bear' constellations. The moth is called a Pine Beauty (Panolis Flammae) — it flies at night in pine woods in Ireland and Britain from March to May, many months earlier than most others.

Astronime Domine

I have been many shapes;
I have journeyed as an eagle;
I have been a boat on the sea;
I have been a director in battle.

Enchanted for a year
In the foam of water.
I have been a poker in a fire;
I have been a tree in a covert.

I know the star knowledge,
Before the Earth was made.
I know the Light whose name is
    splendour

And the number of the ruling
    lights
That scatter rays of fire above the
    deep.

I have travelled, I have made a
    circuit;
I have slept in a hundred islands;
I have dwelt in a hundred cities;
Learned druids
Prophesy ye of Arthur?

(From *Romance of Taliesen*,
translated by D W Nash)

15

Personal attributes:

Patient, reliable, security-loving.
Sometimes possessive, rigid, resentful.

The **Cow** is ruled by the planet Venus.
Its element is Earth. (See p 32.)

Exactly at noon the waves were stirred with a mighty commotion, and three cows rose up from the sea — a white, a red and a black — all beautiful to behold, with sleek skin, large soft eyes, and curved horns, white as ivory. They stood upon the shore for a while, looking around them. Then each one went in a different direction, by three roads: the black one went South, the red went North, and the milk white heifer (the Bó Finn) crossed the plain of Ireland to the very centre where stood the King's palace . . . . In the process of time the white heifer gave birth to twins, a male and a female, and from them descended a great race, still existing in Ireland.'

(From *Ancient Legends of Ireland* by Lady Wilde, 1888)

This is the month of the cow. Cattle have been the subject of veneration in Celtic countries, as elsewhere, since greatest antiquity.

Eurynome was an Orphic moon goddess who became Rhea (Rheo = I flow), the Greek deity whose milk formed the Milky Way. In Ireland Bóinn (Bó Ann) is the white cow whose milk forms the sacred River Boyne.

The significance of milk as a life-giving substance is universal. It endures in the Christian tradition where the milk of the Holy Virgin is a symbol of divine grace. Paradise is known as the Land of Milk and Honey. In Shakespeare's *Merchant of Venice*, reference is made to 'the milk of human kindness'.

As well as Bóinn, another white moon cow exists in the Irish tradition, An Bó Finne (the fair or white cow), who gives the name Bóthar Bó Finne (the track of the white cow) to the Milky Way.

The first three cows emerge from the sea in the west of Ireland.

That cows were sacred in Ireland is attested by the Revd Geoffrey Keating (1570–1650) who, in his renowned *History of Ireland*, mentions that in AD 528 the high king of Ireland was murdered by his eldest son because he had slaughtered a sacred cow. The goddess Bríd is also associated with cows — one of her Scottish titles is 'Tranquil of the Kine'. Cows are still regarded as sacred in India.

17

Personal attributes:

Versatile, adaptable, lively minded.
Sometimes superficial, inconsistent, restless.

The **Serpent** is ruled by the planet Mercury.
Its element is Air. (See p 32.)

St Patrick and the Serpent

There is a lake in one of the Galtee mountains where there is a great serpent chained to a rock, and he may be heard constantly crying out, 'O Patrick, is the Luan, or Monday, long from us?'

For when St Patrick cast this serpent into the lake he bade him be chained to the rock till Lá an Luan (The Day of Judgement). But the serpent mistook the word and thought that the saint meant Luan, Monday.

So he still expects to be freed from one Monday to another, and the clanking of his chains on that day is awful to hear as he strives to break them and get free.

(From *Ancient Legends of Ireland* by Lady Wilde, 1888)

This is the month of the serpent, which appears in many mythological traditions. In the Jewish tradition Moses lifted up a serpent in the desert as a symbol of Yahweh (God the Father), and serpent gods abound in Mayan, Indian and European mythologies. There was even an Ophite (Greek *opis* = snake) Christian sect that honoured the serpent as a symbol of Christ himself.

Though the serpent has become a symbol of corruption in mainstream Christianity, outside of this snakes were a symbol of wisdom and healing. The staff that has endured into modern times as the hallmark of a true physician has a very interesting history, originating in the caduceus of Hermes. The caduceus is a wand surmounted with two wings and entwined by two serpents, which was carried by the Greek herald Hermes, messenger of the gods, and is a symbol of wisdom and healing. The Greek god Aesculapius or Asclepius, a god of healing, a serpent god, also carried a staff with a snake coiled round it. Sacred snakes were kept in the sanctuaries of Aesculapius in the ancient Greek city of Epidaurus and elsewhere. The followers of Aesculapius were physicians, and Hippocrates (*c.* 400 BC) is said to have composed his

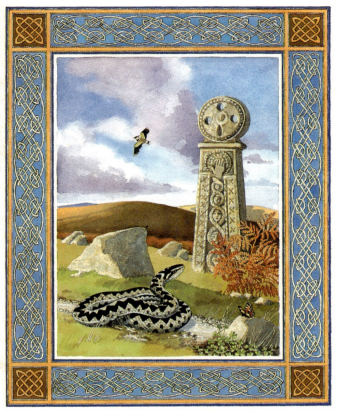

A 10th C. Celtic stone monument showing the symbolic snakes, the Holy Trinity, and the healing hand of God.

treatises from inscriptions he found on the walls of their sacred *sanitorii* or temples.

In Ireland the Celtic equivalent to Aesculapius is Dian Céacht, a figure of the Tuatha De Danann, a people who came originally from Greece. Dian Céacht made a silver hand for the wounded King Nuada, thereafter known as Nuada Airgeadlámh (Silverhand). He also restored the dead to life and was skilled in the use of herbs and all forms of healing.

On another level the serpent is one of the seasonal gods of the year, which take the form of four holy beasts — lion, bull, serpent and eagle. They also represent the four evangelists of the Gospels, with John being represented by the snake.

The banishment of snakes from Ireland by St Patrick is perhaps an allegorical allusion to the establishment of Christianity on the island.

Personal attributes:
Emotional, protective, intuitive.
Sometimes moody, changeable, clinging.

The **Dog** is ruled by the Moon.
Its element is Water (See p 32.)

Culainn the smith speaks to Setanta about the slaying of his guard dog:

'Child,' he said, 'that was a good member of my family you took from me, for he was the protector of my goods and my flocks and my herds and of all that I had.'

Setanta replies: 'If there is a whelp of the same breed to be had in Ireland I will rear and train him until he is as good a hound as the one killed; and until that time I myself will be your watchdog to guard your goods, your cattle and your house.'

'I could have given no better award myself,' said Cathbad the Druid. 'And from this day out your name will be Cú Chullain, the Hound of Culainn.'

'I am better pleased with my own name of Setanta, son of Sualtim,' said the boy.

'Do not say that,' said Cathbad, 'for all the men in the whole world will one day have the name of Cú Chullain in their mouths'.

'If that is so then I am content to keep it,' said the boy.

And this is how he came by the name Cuchullain.

(From *The Boy Deeds of Cuchullain* by Lady Gregory)

This is the month of the dog, an animal with many mythological associations. The myths generally fall into two categories, one where the creature is tame, noble, a friend and protector of humankind, the other where the dog is considered unclean, sinister and very dangerous.

Aesculapius, the Greek deity of physicians, a god of harmony and healing, is usually accompanied by a dog, while the Greek Artemis, the huntress, always has her noble hound at her side. Pluto, the Greek god of the Underworld, has a dog with three heads, called Cerberus, who was stolen by Hercules on one of his descents into that region.

20

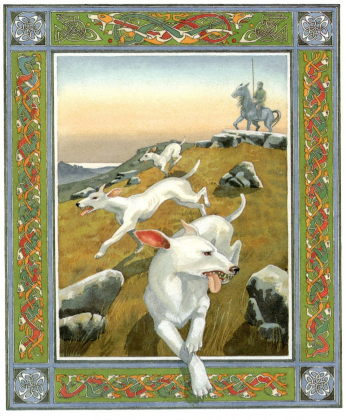

In the Romance of Phyll, *Arawn, king of Anwymon, a pale horse,
appears in pursuit of a stag with his pack of Gabriel hounds —
white, red-eared dogs from Hell. (The stag is a human soul.)*

White, red-eared hounds
appear in both the Welsh
and Irish traditions. In Irish
mythology the hound of
Culainn, slain by the child
Setanta, shares both the dark
and light aspects of canine
nature. Bran, chief hound of
the Fianna and friend and
companion to the warrior
leader Fionn, was the
noblest and most
magnificent hound in
Ireland, leading the Fianna's
three-thousand-strong pack.
Also in the Irish tradition we
often meet the Pooka, the
huge black demon dog from
Hell.

Personal attributes:

Warm-hearted, creative, well organised.
Sometimes patronising, dogmatic, interfering.

The **Cat** is ruled by the Sun.
Its element is Fire. (See p 32.)

*Whoever slays the guardian cat of the king's grain, or steals it, the cat's head to be set on a clean, clear floor and held up by the tail, and wheat to be poured over it until it is covered entirely.**

In Law, the essential qualities of an excellent cat are that it should be sound in eyes, ears, teeth, tail and claws, with all its fur intact; and that it should kill well rats and mice, not eat its own kittens and not be screeching at every full moon.

* This was the forfeit

(From the Welsh Medieval Laws)

This is the month of the cat, a mysterious creature with many mythological associations.

The Egyptians venerated cats above all creatures, and their goddess Bast or Ubast was a feline deity. The killing of a cat was a capital offence until Roman times in Egypt.

There was said to be a cat cult in Ireland in pre-Christian times, and the chief monarch of all the cats in Ireland dwelt in a cave near Clonmacnoise, County Offaly. He was a large, slender black cat with a silver collar and eyes like burning coals, who gave vituperative answers to anyone who tried to deceive him. This King of the Cats appears in folklore as Irusan, son of Arusan, with his wife Spitfire, his daughter Sharp Tooth, and his sons the Purrer and the Growler.

Cats were particularly venerated at the time of winnowing corn, as they

Irusan, son of Arusan, the sarcastic King of the Cats, in his cave near Clonmacnoise.

were responsible for the protection against vermin of grain stores, upon which both animals and humans depended.

Some believed cats to be humans changed by the devil, or even the devil himself. Cats were also guardians of hoards of hidden treasure, and they often had great battles among themselves, which involved every cat in the district.

The fear of and reverence for this enigmatic and beautiful creature can be more easily understood when we realise that cats in the early days were still half-savage and thus potentially very fierce and dangerous.

23

Personal attributes:

Industrious, modest, analytical.
Sometimes fussy, over-critical, conservative.

The **Bee** is ruled by the planet Mercury.
Its element is Earth. (See p 32.)

The early Christian monks lived in beehive-shaped huts in remote areas, symbolising the toil and ultimate sweetness of the hermit's life. This is the prayer of one such monk.

Grant me, Bright Son of the Living God, timeless eternal King of Kings, a quiet dwelling in the heart of your wilderness.

A sweet well of crystal beside it, with water clear and sparkling as the redeeming grace of the Holy Spirit.

A beautiful wood to surround it, to shelter and conceal it, rich home to choirs of birds who sing all day long your praises.

A few companions, humble and mild, to pray to Our Lord.

A small church, with white linen, a dwelling place for the ageless King who moves the ·heavens.

This is the nourishment I would take with gratitude, I would choose none but these: leeks, fragrant and fresh, eggs, warm and wholesome, salmon plump, magnificent, honey from the humming bees.

My need supplied by the King of Most Honour, and myself to be praising Him always, in every place.

(From a medieval Irish prayer, adapted by M Gowen)

This is the month of the bee, of which there are many delightful stories in various traditions. In the Bible Samson's famous riddle 'out of strength came sweetness' was a reference to a swarm of bees that emerged from the carcass of a lion he had killed, leaving wild honey behind. In Greek mythology the first swarm of bees was said to have emerged from a lion killed by Hercules on Mount Pelion.

In Sicily Mount Eryx is famous for the visit of Butes, the bee keeper, son of Boreas (the North Wind).

In Europe witches were said to have the ability to change from a hare to a trout to a bee to a mouse. These animals represent the four seasons.

The bee feeds on midsummer flowers.

In midsummer the queen bee is the goddess about whom the males swarm, and Venus courted her mortal lover Anchises on a mountainside to the humming of bees.

Beehive-shaped tombs were once a symbol of regeneration and fertility.

Paradise is known as the Land of Milk and Honey, the purest and most nourishing of foods, representing the sweetness and mystery of life itself. Bees also represent industry and cooperation, and are universally loved and honoured as one of the most beautiful gifts of the Creator.

25

Personal attributes:

Easy-going, urbane, peaceful.
Sometimes indecisive, self-indulgent, gullible.

The **Pig** is ruled by the planet Venus.
Its element is Air. (See p 32.)

In the Welsh *Romance of Llew*, the Old Sow of Menawr Penardd eats the flesh of Llew, who is restored to life by Gwydion.

Gwydion came under the tree and looked at what the sow was feeding on and he saw she was eating putrid flesh and vermin. Then he looked up . . . and beheld on the top of the tree an eagle, and when the eagle shook itself, there fell vermin and putrid flesh from it, and these the sow devoured. It seemed to him that the eagle was Llew, and he sang:

Oak that grows between two banks;
Darkened is the sky and hill!
Shall I not tell him by his wounds
That this is Llew?

The eagle flew down to the lowest branch of the tree. Gwydion sang again:

Oak that grows beneath the steep;
Stately and majestic in aspect.
Shall I not speak of it
That Llew will come to my lap?

The eagle came and perched on Gwydion's knee. Gwydion struck him with his magic wand so that he returned to his own form.

(From *Romance of Llew*, translated by Lady Charlotte Guest)

This is the month of the pig, which is honoured at the fall of the year. It is thus an animal associated with death.

The Celts honoured the pig, which they regarded as central to their agriculture and their lives. Celtic chieftains were buried with large joints of pork to nourish them on their journey to the Otherworld.

In Egypt, Set, the sun-god, disguised as a boar, killed Osiris, lover of Isis. Apollo, the Greek sun-god, disguised as a boar, killed Adonis, lover of Aphrodite. While in Ireland Fionn mac Cumhaill, disguised as a boar, killed Diarmaid, lover of Gráinne.

Wild boars in the forest.

Pig (Libra)
24 September–23 October

In Celtic times boars were honoured for their valour and courage, and this is the month in which the boar-hunting season began.

Pigs are associated with the moon, as they vary in colour between white, red and black, and have crescent-shaped tusks. Pigs are known to eat the flesh of corpses, and the white goddess Alphito appears as a sow, as does Albina, who gives Albion its name.

Conversely, in Cornwall in England, a white sow called Hen Wen goes about bearing gifts of grain, bees and her own young — she is seen as the bringer of plenty.

Porcus (Latin for 'pig'), or Orcus, was a Roman god of death who gave his name to the Orkney islands.

27

Personal attributes:

Determined, powerful, passionate.
Sometimes secretive, jealous, obsessive.

The **Beetle** is ruled by the planet Mars.
Its element is Water. (See p 32.)

The beetle

The beetle is not killed by the people for the following reason: they have a tradition that one day the chief priests sent messengers in every direction to look for the Lord Jesus, and they came to a field where a man was reaping, and asked him —

'Did Jesus of Nazareth pass this way?'

'No,' said the man, 'I have not seen him.'

'But I know better,' said a little clock running up, 'for he was here today and rested, and has not long gone away.'

'That is false,' said a great big black beetle, coming forward; 'He has not passed since yesterday, and you will never find him on this road; try another.'

So the people kill the clock because he tried to betray Christ; but they spare the beetle and will not touch him, because he saved the Lord on that day.

(From *Ancient Legends of Ireland* by Lady Wilde, 1888)

The beetle is a nocturnal creature, representing the hidden, darker aspects of the mysteries of life.

Beetles breed prolifically, and so are associated with fertility. Their habit of feeding on detritus and dung associates them with death and decay, but also with resurrection, as they perform a very important function at the most basic level of nature.

The deathwatch beetle makes a clicking sound as it burrows through rotten wood or furniture. This sound is said to be an omen of approaching death, but it is actually a mating call. Because of this 'ticking' sound this beetle has been given the affectionate name 'clock' in the Irish tradition, which is also symbolic of the passing of time and the inevitability of death.

The Egyptians honoured the scarab beetle, which is also found in Europe. They regarded this little creature

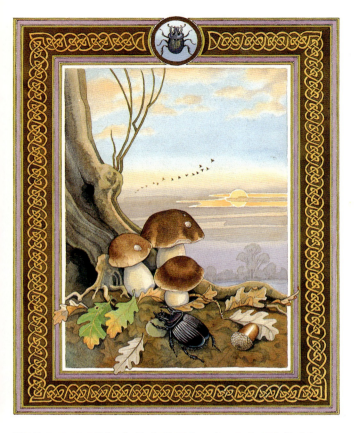

The European scarab beetle. To the Egyptians the scarab symbolised the living Creator, who evolved everything out of matter that he himself had made.

as a symbol of the living
sun-god, Khepera, whose
name means to exist, to
become or to roll — a fitting
name for the sun.

Personal attributes:

Straightforward, philosophical, free-spirited.
Sometimes careless, tactless, irresponsible.

The **Horse** is ruled by the planet Jupiter.
Its element is Fire. (See p 32.)

The ride with the fairies

The fairies take great delight in horsemanship, and are splendid riders. Many fine young men are enticed to ride with them, when they dash along with the fairies like the wind, Finvarra himself leading, on his great black horse with the red nostrils, that look like flames of fire. And ever after the young men are the most fearless riders in the country, so the people know at once that they have hunted with the fairies. And after the hunt some favourite of the party is taken to a magnificent supper in the fairy palace, and when he has drunk of the bright red wine they lull him to sleep with soft music. But never again can he find the fairy palace, and he looks in vain for the handsome horseman on his fine black steed, with all the gay huntsmen in their green velvet dresses, who rushed over the field with him, like a flash of the storm wind. They have passed away for ever from his vision, like a dream of the night.'

(From *Ancient Legends of Ireland* by Lady Wilde, 1888)

This is the month of the horse, a noble and handsome animal who appears throughout the world in myth, legend and folklore.

In Greek mythology we meet the wonderful Pegasus, a winged horse who sprang from the blood of Medusa, the decapitated Gorgon.

In the classical tradition we find that the mare goddess of Troy had three chariots drawn by the twelve sacred horses of Boreas, the North Wind.

In Ireland, Manannán mac Lir had a marvellous horse called Aonbharr, who was as swift as the naked cold wind of spring. Aonbharr was also a sea horse. Finvarra, king of the fairies, rode a great black horse with flaming nostrils, while the sinister Pooka, the huge demon dog from hell, materialised in the shape of a horse.

The Greek mother goddess Demeter, in the shape of a

The Pooka, who materialised in the shape of a black horse.

mare, was pursued and caught by the Greek father god Zeus, in the form of a stallion, while Epona or Rhiannon was the mare goddess of the Celts. Macha was the Irish form of Epona and she gives her name to many places in Ireland, for example Eamhain Mhacha (Navan Fort, County Armagh).

In England, the white horse of Uffingdon and the Silbury horse are linked with these gods, as is the hobby horse — a masked symbolic wooden horse that is ridden by a dancer at Maytime in traditional English folk dances.

Horse (Sagittarius)
23 November–21 December

31

Compatibility Guide

The **DEER** is ruled by the planet Saturn. Its element is Earth.

Deer people can expect harmonious relations with other Earth signs (Cow and Bee). Deer people will also relate well to Water signs (Dog, Beetle and Fish).

Difficulties may be expected in relation to Air signs (Pig, Heron and Serpent) and Fire signs (Bear, Cat and Horse).

The **BEAR** is ruled by the planet Mars. Its element is Fire.

Bear people can expect harmonious relations with other Fire signs (Cat and Horse). Bear people will also relate well to Air signs (Pig, Heron and Serpent).

Difficulties may be expected in relation to Earth signs (Deer, Cow and Bee) and Water signs (Dog, Beetle and Fish).

The **HERON** is ruled by the planet Uranus. Its element is Air.

Heron people can expect harmonious relations with other Air signs (Serpent and Pig). Heron people will also relate well to Fire signs (Bear, Cat and Horse).

Difficulties may be expected in relation to Earth signs (Deer, Cow and Bee) and Water signs (Dog, Beetle and Fish).

The **COW** is ruled by the planet Venus. Its element is Earth.

Cow people can expect harmonious relations with other Earth signs (Deer and Bee). Cow people will also relate well to Water signs (Dog, Beetle and Fish).

Difficulties may be expected in relation to Air signs (Pig, Heron and Serpent) and Fire signs (Bear, Cat and Horse).

The **FISH** is ruled by the planet Neptune. Its element is Water.

Fish people can expect harmonious relations with other Water signs (Dog and Beetle). Fish people will also relate well to Earth signs (Deer, Cow and Bee).

Difficulties may be expected in relation to Air signs (Pig, Heron and Serpent) and Fire signs (Bear, Cat and Horse).

The **SERPENT** is ruled by the planet Mercury. Its element is Air.

Serpent people can expect harmonious relations with other Air signs (Pig and Heron). Serpent people will also relate well to Fire signs (Bear, Cat and Horse).

Difficulties may be expected in relation to Earth signs (Deer, Cow and Bee) and Water signs (Dog, Beetle and Fish).

The **DOG** is ruled by the Moon. Its element is Water.
Dog people can expect harmonious relations with other Water signs (Beetle and Fish). Dog people will also relate well to Earth signs (Deer, Cow and Bee).
Difficulties may be expected in relation to Air signs (Pig, Heron and Serpent) and Fire signs (Bear, Cat and Horse).

The **CAT** is ruled by the Sun. Its element is Fire.
Cat people can expect harmonious relations with other Fire signs (Horse and Bear). Cat people will also relate well to Air signs (Pig, Heron and Serpent).
Difficulties may be expected in relation to Earth signs (Deer, Cow and Bee) and Water signs (Dog, Beetle and Fish).

The **BEE** is ruled by the planet Mercury. Its element is Earth.
Bee people can expect harmonious relations with other Earth signs (Cow and Deer). Bee people also relate well to Water signs (Dog, Beetle and Fish).
Difficulties are to be expected in relation to Air signs (Pig, Heron and Serpent) and Fire signs (Bear, Cat and Horse).

The **PIG** is ruled by the planet Venus. Its element is Air.
Pig people can expect harmonious relations with other Air signs (Heron and Serpent). Pig people will also relate well to Fire signs (Bear, Cat and Horse).
Difficulties may be expected in relation to Earth signs (Deer, Cow and Bee) and Water signs (Dog, Beetle and Fish).

The **BEETLE** is ruled by the planet Mars. Its element is Water.
Beetle people can expect harmonious relations with other Water signs (Fish and Dog). Beetle people will also relate well to Earth signs (Deer, Cow and Bee).
Difficulties may be expected in relation to Air signs (Pig, Heron and Serpent) and Fire signs (Bear, Cat and Horse).

The **HORSE** is ruled by the planet Jupiter. Its element is Fire.
Horse people can expect harmonious relations with other Fire signs (Cat and Bear). Horse people will also relate well to Air signs (Pig, Heron and Serpent).
Difficulties may be expected in relation to Earth signs (Deer, Cow and Bee) and Water signs (Dog, Beetle and Fish).

Glossary

Beth-Luis-Nion: This is the name given to the old Celtic tree calendar, which consisted of thirteen months and one day. Beth, Luis and Nion are the Goidelic or Gaelic names for the trees birch, rowan and ash, which belonged to the first three months of the tree calendar. The letters B, L and N are also the first three consonants of the ogham alphabet.

Fianna: A band of legendary warriors led by Fionn Mac Cumhaill.

Great Flood (Deluge): Legends of a Great Flood exist in all traditions. The biblical Deluge was substituted by medieval scholars in an effort to reconcile the Judeo-Christian tradition with the older one.

Milesians: A legendary race of people said to have their origins in the city of Miletus in Asia Minor. According to the celebrated Irish historian Revd Geoffrey Keating, the Milesians came to Ireland from Spain c. 3000 BC and defeated the Tuatha De Danann, who then went to live beneath the mountains, rivers and lakes of Ireland, where they still live and emerge frequently as the 'Sídhe' or fairies.

Ogham: An ancient Celtic alphabet of straight lines meeting or crossing the edge of a stone. It is the accepted Irish tradition that this alphabet came from Greece through Spain, and it was widely used in pre-Roman Britain and in Ireland.

Ollav (Ollamh) poet: Chief poet and druid. In Ireland he or she had to be a doctor of civil law, philosophy, ancient and current languages, skilled in music, augury, divinity, mathematics, astronomy, medicine, geography, and temporal and metaphysical history.

Sanskrit: An ancient Indian language used for over three thousand years. All ancient Indian sacred texts were written in Sanskrit, for example, the *Upanisads* and the *Bhagavad Gita*. All contemporary north Indian languages derived from Sanskrit, and many Sanskrit words are to be found in Celtic languages, for example, *skt dwr* becomes *duir* in old Irish and *doras* in modern Irish.

Tuatha De Danann: The people of the goddess Danu, who went to live underground after they were defeated by the Milesians. The Tuatha De Danann still live under the mountains, rivers and lakes of Ireland, and emerge frequently to hunt, steal babies and beautiful young girls, turn milk sour, and generally confuse and torment people.